To

_____

From

_____

Date

_____

I Will Change Your Name

I Will Change Your Name

*Messages from the Father
to a Heart Broken by Divorce*

by Dana Hood

LEAFWOOD
PUBLISHERS

I Will Change Your Name

Messages from the Father to a Heart Broken by Divorce

Copyright 2007 by Dana Hood

ISBN 978-0-89112-509-9

Printed in the United States of America

Cover and interior design by Greg Jackson, Thinkpen Design, llc

For information contact:
Leafwood Publishers, Abilene, Texas
1-877-816-4455 toll free
www.leafwoodpublishers.com

07 08 09 10 11 12 / 7 6 5 4 3 2 1

Table of Contents

Introduction

I don't know what compelled me to ask the question on that night. I had asked many other questions. "Are you alright?" "Did I do something to make you angry?" "Are you tired?" "What's wrong? Are things stressful at work?" But on this night I found myself asking the true question. The one I never let become real in my head or heart before it became real in my voice. "Are you going to leave me?" The words surprised me as they came out of my mouth.

Perhaps the question surprised him too and that's why he hesitated just long enough for me to know the answer—he was seriously considering leaving our marriage. "I'm not happy," he said, "and I am not in love with you anymore." With those words I thought my world would fall apart.

For the next eight months I waited for his final decision. I have never felt so helpless or powerless. We lived in the same house, but clearly not together. Each day I got up, went to work, took care of the kids, and then at night when the house was quiet I would go into my room and close the door. Down the hall behind closed doors was my husband. And I was alone . . . but not really alone.

The Lord made his loving presence known to me during that time in a way I had never experienced before. He spoke sweet messages to my heart through his word, through songs, and through precious brothers and sisters in Christ. Very early in this process it became clear that these messages from the Father's heart were not mine alone, but messages he was calling me to share.

Two weeks after the fateful question, I was invited to speak at the Pepperdine University lectures. Of all things, I was asked talk about nurturing faith in children. How in the world could I accept this invitation when my life was in such a mess? I mean this topic was about family and my family was falling apart. Surely the Lord would want someone who had it all together to accept this call.

I sought the advice of wise pastors. I asked my friends what they thought. I went to my parents for their advice. Every person I talked to said, "Yes! Go! You have something to share! But keep praying about it and see what the Lord leads you to do." Well this was certainly not the answer I wanted. The reason I kept going to more and more people was because I was hoping to get a confirmation of my fears and doubts. I wanted a "NO!" not a "Yes."

You might wonder if I took their advice and prayed about it. Well, of course I did. But I confess that my prayers had a bit of a Moses quality about them. "Lord, surely you don't intend for me to do this. Father, please show me clearly that this is not the time for me to speak for you. Dear God, why did I get this call now? Now that I am so broken.

Now that I have nothing to share."

When none of these strategies presented the closed door I was so desperately seeking I thought of one more sure-fire way to get out of this. I went into my room, held my closed Bible in front of me and prayed, "Lord, I feel really silly doing this. But here I go! I am going to open the Bible and the first verse I read will be my answer." Now I have never done this before and it isn't a strategy I recommend. I am even a little embarrassed to share this with you. But when the pages fell open, the first words my eyes focused on were these. "Commit to the Lord whatever you do and your plans will succeed" (Proverbs 16:2).

So the next day I called and accepted the invitation and later that week I had a reservation for a plane ticket. I was on my way to California and I was scared! In my profession I speak to large groups all the time. It is something I usually love to do. But this time I was petrified. And just as the Lord took care of a fearful Moses by providing Aaron, the Lord provided for me. Four of my dearest friends in the world took that trip with me. They didn't go to hear any other speakers. They went just to sit in the room while I spoke and to pray for me. What an amazing gift is the Body of Christ! I would have never made it without them.

But I did make it. I made my speeches through many tears. Never before had I felt so supported and loved as I looked out at the audience and into the faces of my four dear friends. And never before had I felt more strongly the presence of God's Spirit in my words.

When I finished my last session a woman I had never met before and have never seen again approached me. She put her hands on mine and said, "I don't know what is going on in your life right now, but I can tell you are walking through something very difficult. What I want you to know is that it is because of this that you spoke so powerfully. Thank you for having the courage to do this."

Courage! That was funny. I was petrified. Literally quaking in my shoes. Any strength I had to speak wasn't mine it was the Lord's. That's when I got it. That was the point. It was in my brokenness that the Lord was able to use me. It wasn't about me. It was about him. I would love to tell you that I learned this lesson completely and perfectly from that point, but I confess that it is a lesson the Lord keeps reminding me of.

A few months later when my husband had moved out of the house but had not yet filed for divorce, another invitation came. A colleague asked me to speak to some university students at a young women's spiritual retreat. The theme of the day was "I Will Change Your Name." She asked me to share with these young women how God was changing my name in the midst of the struggle. Before I could offer an excuse she said, "I think there is value in hearing what God is doing while people are still in the middle, not just at the end."

When I began my talk that day, the words caught in my throat and I couldn't speak. Moved by the spirit, my friend came and placed her hands on me and prayed God's peace over me. Once again, I was sustained by prayer. The words then poured through me, but they also poured over me. The Lord was truly changing my name. From abandoned to welcomed. From rejected to cherished. From defeated to victorious.

And he continues this amazing transforming work in my life. At times I listen to the deceiver's lies and forget my name. But the Father is always there to remind me of my true identity. I am his. His cherished bride.

And so it is with you. If you will call on him, he will change your name too. What are the names that you carry? Lonely? Abandoned? Bitter? Hopeless? Weary? Go to the Father. Let him speak your true name into your heart.

My prayer is that the messages that I share in this book will indeed be messages from the Father to your broken heart. I am sure that many parts of our stories are different, but we share a common grief. We also share a common hope. It is this hope, the hope "that does not disappoint us," that has guided me through the valley. It will guide you too and I am honored and humbled to walk along with you for a time through the pages of this book.

God's blessings to you, precious child of God.

Dana

DAY 1

Longing for Reality

But You, O LORD, are a shield about me,
My glory, and the One who lifts my head.

PSALM 3:3

He looked at me and said, "I am not in love with you anymore.
I'm not sure I want to be married to you anymore." And with those
words my world fell apart. I knew that things weren't great, but I
thought we would always be married. Maybe not happily, but
always married. This couldn't be real!

As I went through the next day, I knew I was walking, but it
seemed that my feet never really touched the ground. It was as if I
weren't real. I touched but couldn't feel. I listened but couldn't hear.
I spoke but the words seemed to come from someone else. It was all
a blur. I longed for reality. Something I could hold onto.

The Lord surrounded me on that day and the days that
followed. He provided for me a shield to hold onto. He did indeed
lift my head. He was my voice, my breath, the strength in my legs.

Gradually, the Lord gave me a new reality—His reality. He restored my joy and spoke His peace into my heart. And on those days when the grief returns, often unexpectedly, I look to Him, my shield, my glory, the One who lifts my head.

Holy Lord, thank you
for being my reality.

Day 2

The God Who Sees Me

O Lord, You have searched me and known me.
You know when I sit down and when I rise up;
You understand my thought from afar.

PSALM 139:1

She was not a close friend. We attended the same monthly Bible study and visited on occasion. I respected her, admired her, but we weren't close friends. So it was especially meaningful that God chose her.

My husband had just told me he was seriously considering leaving our marriage. I had told two or three of my closest friends, but no one else. But she came to me that night and said, "The Lord has put it on my heart to be praying for you."

I couldn't believe it. She couldn't have known. She didn't know. I believe God chose her for precisely this reason. It was His powerful and gentle way of saying, "I am here. I know. I haven't forgotten you."

I love the story of Hagar, when she runs away to the desert to escape Sarah's jealousy. There alone in the desert, the Lord came to her. He made it clear that she was not abandoned. And there in that lonely place, she came to know the "God who sees me."

He sees you too and has not abandoned you. He has searched you and knows you. You are not alone.

All-knowing Father, thank you
for knowing me completely
and loving me anyway.

DAY 3

Holy Hands

And a leper came to Jesus, beseeching Him and falling on his knees
before Him, and saying, "If You are willing, You can make me clean."
Moved with compassion, Jesus stretched out His hand and
touched him, and said to him, "I am willing; be cleansed."

MARK 1:40-41

I never cease to be moved by this story. Jesus touched the untouchable. Lepers were outcasts, living alone in their pain, and labeled "unclean." Through no fault of their own, they were rejected by a world that feared them. And so it was with this man—a leper crying out for healing.

Jesus could have healed this man from a distance. But "moved with compassion" he touched him. Can you imagine it? Picture the leper as his body shudders with the emotion of that first touch in perhaps a very long time. Do you see the tears fall from his pain-filled eyes? Close your eyes and listen to the groans of overwhelming joy as this precious child of God felt the healing touch of the one who loved him fully—loved him best. What a holy moment!

I have come to understand the power of touch even more since the death of my marriage. Rejected, alone, and feeling labeled by my divorce, I cried out and Jesus sent people to be His hands. They massaged my feet, held me while I wept, and rubbed lotion on my tear-stained face. These were holy moments too. I was touched by Jesus.

Perhaps you have experienced the healing power of touch at a time when you were walking through grief—perhaps not. Touch is a funny thing, though. When we touch others, we are touched as well. Look for opportunities to be the hands of Jesus and touch others with healing, holy hands. You will be amazed at how blessed you will be.

Father, help me be the hands of Jesus today.

DAY 4

Nowhere to Hide

Let us hold fast the confession of our hope without wavering,
for He who promised is faithful; and let us consider how to stimulate one
another to love and good deeds, not forsaking our own assembling
together, as is the habit of some, but encouraging one another;
and all the more as you see the day drawing near.

HEBREWS 10:23-25

Before I walked through the death of my marriage I thought that church would be a place of comfort for a person in grief. What I discovered instead was that church was often the most difficult and painful place to be. I suddenly found myself wanting to avoid Sunday mornings—to hide at home because at church there was nowhere to hide.

Often words spoken from the pulpit or written in the church bulletin seemed like a big spotlight shining directly on the parts of my life that weren't what they were supposed to be. And there was nowhere to hide.

It was impossible to pretend when I met the Lord at the

communion table. Sharing the body and the blood made me look deep into my soul and there was nowhere to hide.

So why did I keep going? My children. They needed to be there. I couldn't let what was happening between me and their dad separate them from their church family. One Sunday I was sitting with my daughter. Fortunately she had invited a friend to sit with us so she was focused on her and not on me. I don't remember why but suddenly I panicked. I had to get out. I looked down the aisle at a friend and she saw the desperation in my eyes. She nodded—a silent message that she would watch my daughter.

I don't know where I was going. I just wanted to hide. Out of the auditorium. Through the foyer. Down the hall. And then I felt it. A hand on my shoulder. I turned to see the face of one of our church elders. He opened his arms and I fell in. It was for a moment a place to hide. Finally I calmed and he gently led me back into the assembly.

I learned that day that there truly is nowhere to hide from grief except in the arms of the Savior and often His arms take the form of His church. Don't forsake the assembly.

Lord, keep calling me back to you and back into community with your people. And when I run to hide, send someone after me.

DAY 5

I Am the Water

When you pass through the waters, I will be with you;
And through the rivers, they will not overflow you. When you walk
through the fire, you will not be scorched, nor will the flame burn you.

ISAIAH 43:2

I have learned so much about God's constant presence during the last two years as I have walked through the death of my marriage. The Lord has given me many clear reminders of His care and faithfulness.

There is one night, however, that stands out from the rest as a marker for me. I was spending an evening with my ladies' prayer group. We were celebrating a birthday that night with an evening in the pool and hot tub. Everyone else had left the pool and chosen to relax in the hot tub. That left me alone with the Lord in the water.

He spoke to me powerfully and gently that night. He said, "I am the water—gently rocking you as you float and softly flowing over your skin. Just lie back. I will hold you up. I am the water." Later I began to swim some laps and the Father spoke again. "I am the water and sometimes you can float, but sometimes you have to swim. There are meetings to attend, classes to teach, and children to care for. You have to pull with your arms and kick your legs. But even then, I am the water. If I were not there, you would be thrashing against the ground. So whether your are resting and floating or swimming with everything you have, remember, I am the water."

I will never forget that night. It was a precious gift to me from a loving Father who will not let the waters overflow me or let me be burned in the fire. He will carry me. And He will carry you. He is the water.

Lord, thank You for Your constant presence.

DAY 6

I Learned to Pray in Kindergarten

It is good to give thanks to the LORD
and to sing praises to Your name, O Most High;
To declare Your loving kindness in the morning
and Your faithfulness by night.

PSALM 92:1-2

One of my favorite things about children is the way they pray. Little kids don't think there is anything too silly or too small to talk about with God. Consider this sweet simple prayer of one of my kindergarten buddies.

Dear God,

Thank you for corn and flowers. Thank you that I got to go swimming today. Thank you for mountains and for my two friends in my class and their names are John and Patrick. Thank you for sharing our bones with us cuz without them we would flop over.

Amen

There was a time in my journey through divorce when giving thanks did not come very easily. There had been so much loss. It didn't seem I had anything to be thankful for.

It was during this difficult time that I rediscovered the power of child-like prayer. In my prayers I began thanking God for everything— my toes and fingers, my favorite pillow, flowers and corn.

It was amazing how God blessed these simple prayers. It really is good to give thanks to the Lord! Spend some time thanking Him today for the little things. You might discover that they aren't so little after all.

Father, thank you!

DAY 7

Just Two Little Bottles

You are not to say, "It is a conspiracy!
In regard to all that this people call a conspiracy,
And you are not to fear what they fear or be in dread of it.
It is the LORD of hosts whom you should regard as holy.
And He shall be your fear, and He shall be your dread.

ISAIAH 8:12-13

I admit it. I caved in on December 29, 1999 and actually bought some bottled water to prepare for Y2K. It was only two little bottles. It was the possibility of embarrassment if I had been wrong all along and all those people panicking were actually right that made me do it. Okay, there was maybe a little tiny bit of concern, well, maybe something sort of like fear that this thing really was going to cause some catastrophic situations. I don't know why I thought two liters of bottled water would help. (I was too embarrassed to buy more.)

I was pretty amazed, though, as I watched the response of people, even Christians, as they prepared for months ahead of time for disaster. Somehow I thought, "The Lord will provide. Even if people do think computers control the world—God is in control here." I saw people of faith being caught up by fear.

The Lord tells us that we do not have to fear the things the world fears. We shouldn't be troubled by the conspiracies of our time. God is holy and He is in control. We can place our trust in Him—the kind of trust that doesn't even require the purchase of two little bottles of water.

Lord of all we see, remind me today that no matter what, You are still in control.

DAY 8

Could Be Worse!

Therefore we do not lose heart, but though our outer man is decaying,
yet our inner man is being renewed day by day. For momentary, light
affliction is producing for us an eternal weight of glory far beyond all
comparison, while we look not at the things which are seen,
but the things which are not see are eternal.

2 CORINTHIANS 4:16-18

My husband was still living in the house. The words had been spoken. He wasn't in love with me any more. He wasn't happy. He didn't want to talk about it. Don't ask him any questions. He slept down the hall and we spoke only when it was necessary. I knew that he would eventually leave.

This was one of the darkest, most difficult times of my life. I lived each day not knowing whether the morning would bring the end of my marriage. I was so alone, so afraid. I was definitely losing heart and my outer man was in serious decay.

I called a friend and asked her to go with me to a movie. I just needed to get out of the house and escape for a while. So we looked through the movie ads and tried to find a suitable choice. Romance was definitely out. A tearjerker might get me crying and I wouldn't be able to stop. Comedy? I didn't think I would find anything funny. So we settled on nail-biting suspense. The movie? "The Edge."

At one point in the movie two men sit alone, stranded at the top of an icy mountain after a plane crash. They have no food, no weapons, no means of shelter, and less than adequate clothing. The main character knows that his companion is having an affair with his wife and suspects that he is attempting to kill him. They are being stalked by a crazed grizzly bear that has already killed one of their friends.

This is supposed to be a very serious moment in the movie, but suddenly I found myself laughing. I turned to my friend and said, "See, my life could be worse!" While this might sound silly to you, it was a very profound moment for me. In that moment I could see that my affliction was light and momentary. And somehow that became a marker for me in times when I couldn't—when I, like Paul, "despaired even of life." That unexpected moment reminded me that when my life is falling apart, God renews my spirit.

Father, when what I see brings me despair, help me
set my eyes on your eternal weight of glory.

DAY 9

Like a Child

Truly I say to you, whoever does not receive the
kingdom of God like a child will not enter it at all.

MARK 10:15

Have you ever wondered what Jesus meant by this? I mean children are so . . . childish! Isn't the point of life to eventually become a grown-up? But I think we have missed the point. Jesus isn't telling us to be childish. He is telling us to receive like a child.

Think about it. Children aren't afraid to ask for what they need. "I have a hurt, Mommy. Will you kiss it?" They aren't afraid to admit it when they need help, "I'm scared. Can I sleep with you?" Children know they have a lot of growing up to do. "When I get big, I am going to be just like you." Kids haven't lost the ability to be caught up in the wonder of life. "Look Daddy, it is a big rainbow!"

Think about yourself. Have you grown up a little too much? Have you forgotten how to receive God's good gifts? Life has become ordinary and you go from day to day taking care of things all by yourself. You are missing out on the blessings that the Lord is just waiting to give you if you will only forget some of the "important" and "grown-up" things you know. Stop. Reach out your hand like a child and receive.

Loving and patient Father, thank you for looking past the grown-up in me and loving the child I have forgotten how to be.

DAY 10

Tuck Me In

In the day of my trouble I sought the Lord;
In the night my hand was stretched out without weariness;
My soul refused to be comforted.

On that night I went to my room, closed my door, climbed into an empty bed and tried to sleep. My husband was down the hall behind a locked door and I was alone. Alone with my thoughts. Alone with my fears. Alone with my God.

I spent night after night crying, praying, and writing in my journal. There were many nights sleep wouldn't come. My soul really "refused to be comforted." That night was no different.

I was weary in body, mind and spirit. I desperately needed to sleep. So I stretched out my hand and prayed. "Lord, I have to sleep. My kids need me. My students need me. I need me. I can't do this tonight. I have to sleep. So Father, I'm waiting. I need you to tuck me in."

The Lord answered my prayer that night. His peace came over me and I felt His comforting presence like a mother pulling the blankets up around my shoulders. There with my precious Father, I slept.

Does your soul refuse to be comforted? Stretch out your hand. His hand will be there waiting.

Father, thank you for being a God who does not love us from afar. Remind me of your presence today.

DAY 11

Simple Faith

Learn to do good; seek justice, reprove the ruthless, defend the orphan, plead for the widow. Come now, and let us reason together, says the LORD, though your sins are as scarlet, they will be as white as snow; though they are red like crimson, they will be like wool.

ISAIAH 1:17-18

Why do we make religion so complicated? I know that Satan loves to distract us with meaningless issues. Who gets to be on that committee? How should we sing in worship? Should a minister make that much money? We have never done it that way before. I am not sure it's okay.

All the while, God is saying, "It is not that complicated. Love each other. Take care of people who don't have anyone. Listen and learn of me. Give me your heart. I will cleanse you of all your sins."

Satan wants to distract us with disagreements and with questions that will never be completely settled. So we work and we argue and we discuss these difficult issues. All along there are people hurting and injustices being committed and where are we? We are doing the complicated work of religion.

Isn't it amazing though, that the God who created the universe, the One who is beyond human understanding, has made true faith so simple—not easy—but simple.

Father, help me to go about doing the hard work
today of living and loving simply.

Living Above the Label

For the Lord GOD helps me, therefore,
I am not disgraced; therefore, I have set my face like flint,
And I know that I will not be ashamed.

ISAIAH 50:7

I hate the word "divorce." Mostly I hate that it is a word that describes me. Now when I fill out forms I have to mark that spot under "marital status." It makes me feel like I should be wearing a big "D" on my clothes. I feel labeled and disgraced.

But the Lord doesn't let me stay there long. He reminds me that while this is my experience, it isn't my identity. My identity is in the Lord. No matter what has happened, He will remove my shame and I will not be disgraced.

I love the phrase, "I have set my face like a flint." It reminds me of Scarlet O'Hara and her "Never go hungry again!" speech. I stand

and say, "I am not disgraced!" This isn't because I am so brave or even that I am worthy. It is because the "Lord God helps me. . . I will not be ashamed."

Father, thank you for helping me live above
any labels that the world might give me.
Remind me that my true identity is in You.

Day 13

Such a Trooper

*"I feel compassion for the people because they have remained
with Me now three days and have nothing to eat. If I send them
away hungry to their homes, they will faint on the way;
and some of them have come from a great distance."*

MARK 8:2-3

Have you ever been at the end of your rope? Do you remember
a time when you thought you might faint if you had to take another
step? It is easy at times like this to fear that Jesus will lose patience
with us—that He wants you to just pull yourself together. But just
as Jesus looked at these tired, hungry people and felt compassion
for them, He knows when you truly cannot go any farther and with
the same compassion, He wants to take care of your needs.

I came to understand this amazing compassion a few months
ago when the grief over my divorce had become so deep I could not
seem to be comforted. I couldn't think. I could hardly work. I was so
overwhelmed. At that frustrating time some friends who had a little

girl about eighteen months old came to visit. This little girl was something else. She was cheerful and flexible as her parents drug her all over the place with no time to rest. But after two days of this crazy schedule, she lost it. She had reached her limit. Her mother was trying to calm her while she continued to cry and throw her body around. It is easy to get frustrated with a child who is acting like this, but her mother held her gently and said, "I can't really be mad at her, she has been such a trooper."

Later that night I was spending some time in prayer and my thoughts returned this little girl flailing about at the end of her rope. Then the Lord changed the picture in my mind's eye. The little girl became me in the arms of Jesus, crying and refusing to be comforted. And He looked down and said, "I can't be mad at her, she has been such a trooper."

I came to understand that Jesus knows when I have no strength of my own left. At these times he doesn't get fed up with me. He doesn't get angry. He holds me and he waits until I don't need to scream any more.

Father, thank you for holding us while we rest—
and for holding us while we scream.

You've Got to Be Kidding!

"For if you forgive others for their transgressions,
your heavenly Father will also forgive you. But if you do not forgive
others, then your Father will not forgive your transgressions."

MATTHEW 6:14-16

You have got to be kidding! Surely my ex-husband didn't count as one of the "others" that I have to forgive. I didn't know how to do this. The grief was still too fresh, the hurt still too raw. But there it was. I had to find a way to forgive him if I wanted to rest in God's forgiveness.

This seemed impossible. All I could picture was the typical quick conversation of apology that we have all experienced many times. Someone tells us they are sorry and we respond with, "It's alright." But this wasn't alright! My life had been turned upside-down. My children were confused. Besides, he hadn't said he was sorry. Add to that the fact that I wanted to stay angry. I deserved to stay angry. Forgiving my ex-husband not only seemed impossible, I flat did not want to do it.

Still it was there. Forgive. I prayed that the Lord would give me the power to do what seemed impossible—that he would help me understand this completely unrealistic expectation of His! The Lord heard my angry, desperate, and more than a little rebellious prayer.

Under duress, I attended a divorce recovery workshop. Guess what! I wasn't the only divorced person struggling with this forgiveness thing. Turns out it is pretty common. That night I heard a definition of forgiveness that made sense to me. "To forgive means that I give up the right to hurt someone because they hurt me." Wow! That I could do! It was a small but tangible step I could take on this journey of forgiveness. I could let go of my right to take revenge. I could do this for my children. I could do this for the Father. And in the end the Lord taught me that I was doing it for myself too.

Father, thank you for being patient
as I learn to forgive like you.

DAY 15

Something New

Do not call to mind the former things, or ponder things of the past.
Behold, I will do something new, now it will spring forth;
Will you not be aware of it? I will even make a roadway
in the wilderness, rivers in the desert.

ISAIAH 43:18-19

Our God is a God of surprises. New beginnings are His best thing. He is the original recycler. He does His best work when things look the worst. The Israelites were trapped with a sea on one side and their enemies on the other. Surprise! Three men are thrown into a fiery furnace to die. Surprise! The tomb is sealed and the stone closes the door. This was the best surprise.

Could you use a little of God's recycling? Are you walled in by your past? Have you been thrown into the fire of grief and you can't seem to find a way out? Does it seem that your future has been sealed because of former things?

Well, don't give up. This may be the time when God will do His best work in your life. He may not do what you originally thought you wanted. It will almost surely be something you don't expect. But who expects to find a brand new river in the middle of the desert? Place your trust in Him. Give Him your past and walk into His future. You are sure to be surprised.

Holy God, help me stop living my yesterdays.
I give you today and trust you with tomorrow.

DAY 16

All Choked Up!

"And others are the ones on whom seed was sown among the thorns;
these are the ones who have heard the word, but the worries of the world,
and the deceitfulness of riches, and the desires for other things enter in
and choke the word, and it becomes unfruitful."

MARK 4:18-19

I have lots of friends who love to work in the garden. They water and weed and plant and fertilize. They amaze me as they rattle off the names of hundreds of different flowers and plants. I, on the other hand, am a serious threat to anything green. There have been many times that I have disproved a well-meaning florist's words, "You just can't kill it!" If plants were not attached by the roots, they would run when they see me coming.

Don't get me wrong. I am blessed by the beauty of gardens. They are a testimony to God's creativity, attention to detail and love for variety. I just can't make one grow. So I don't usually get the spiritual metaphors of the garden. But this one I get. I can understand thorns.

Will the child support check come in time? I'm not supposed to be divorced. Will I always be single? Will my kids recover from this? Mommy, why did Daddy leave? Thorns! Thorns! Thorns!

I long for the good soil. But I am stuck at the roots. Okay, here I go with a gardening metaphor. A plant can't dig itself up and move to a better flowerbed. That is the work of the gardener. Are you like me? Are you in serious need of a visit from the gardener? Do you need to surrender your thorns so that He can peel them away? Don't keep living in your "choked up" world. Lay your worries at the Master's feet and He will make you flourish and grow.

Father, I give you my worries today. Remind me to give them to you again tomorrow.

DAY 17

Upside-down World

Woe to those who call evil good, and good evil;
Who substitute darkness for light and light for darkness;
Who substitute bitter for sweet and sweet for bitter!

ISAIAH 5:20

One of the best things that has ever happened to my family was to decide not to get cable again when my children and I moved after my divorce. I would like to say that I intentionally and prayerfully decided to remove the influence of television from my home. The truth is that I was just too cheap. That hook-up fee and the monthly payment just seemed like such a big chunk. I was also too lazy to figure out how to get reception through the antenna so that we could watch local channels. So for a long time we were exclusively a VCR family.

During this VCR time of our lives I went to a conference and stayed in a hotel and was quickly sucked in by the channel changer. It was just like riding a bike. You don't forget how to surf channels.

Well, it happened to be at the time of day when those talk shows are on. You know, the ones with "real-life" people with "real-life" stories to tell. As I watched, I was amazed at how upside down our world is. Morality is immoral. Truth is a lie. The perverted is normal.

This indeed is a time when people call the darkness light and evil good. And so it is up to us to be light in darkness. We must live the truth that the world does not believe exists. We do this not as some political crusade; we do this because we know the consequences of living in darkness. The stakes are high because those really are "real-life" people with "real-life" stories who need a "real-life" Savior.

Lord, let your light and your truth
shine through me today.

DAY 18

Only God

Stop regarding man, whose breath of life is in his nostrils;
For why should he be esteemed?

ISAIAH 2:22

I had avoided it for two years. Every six months or so the sign would go up again and I would pass by it at least once a day. And pass by I did. The last thing I wanted to do was to go to a divorce recovery class! But this time it was different. The Lord seemed to be telling me to go.

Now, don't get me wrong. I am pretty stubborn. It wasn't until the second week of the series after my mom casually asked if I had seen the sign and after a friend called me and asked me to go with her that I was finally obedient. I guess God is pretty stubborn too. He wanted me there because He had something to tell me.

I will never forget the words. "No one but God has the right to deem you worthy or unworthy. When you allow someone to determine your worth you are allowing them to play God in your life." Wow! Those words pierced my heart. It was time for me to stop letting my ex-husband determine my value. My value is in the Lord. He has made me worthy.

What about you? Have you let someone in your life play the role of God? Stop regarding man. It is God who should be esteemed and He loves you as you are, right now. Because of Him, you are worthy and no person can change that.

Eternal loving Father, thank you for making this unworthy woman worthy through your love.

They are Playing Our Song!

Behold, God is my salvation, I will trust and not be afraid;
For the LORD GOD is my strength and song,
And He has become my salvation

ISAIAH 12:2

I am amazed by the power of songs. Olympic medalists are overcome with emotion when they hear the playing of their national anthems. You hear a song from your youth and you are back in time. There is that song that you just can't get out of your head. Two young lovers look at each other and say, "They are playing our song." Our emotions swell as the music in a movie draws us into the drama that is unfolding before us. A baby drifts off to sleep as her mother sings a lullaby over her.

Music speaks to our hearts in a way that words cannot. My spirituality is strengthened, challenged, expressed, and directed more often through songs than through almost anything else. And so the thought of God as my song moves me in a way that is beyond words.

Zephaniah tells us that God sings over us. He sings in times of victory. His songs remind us of His faithfulness in the past. Sometimes He sings and sings and sings until we finally stop and listen. He sings songs of love and He sings songs of comfort.

When you feel alone or defeated, don't be afraid. Stop and listen! He is playing your song.

Precious Father, help me hear your song
in the midst of my noisy life today.

Garden Moments

And He was saying, "Abba, Father! All things are possible for You;
remove this cup from Me; yet not what I will, but what You will."

MARK 14:36

Have you ever wondered why God chose to tell us about this
struggle that Jesus had in the garden? Why did He want us to know
that Jesus was afraid and that He hoped for a way out? The Father
lets us see here a Jesus who is fully human; a man alone in his
confusion and agony. Perhaps the Lord wanted us to know that
when we face our own garden moments, Jesus would understand. I
have faced a few garden moments myself—times when I didn't
think I could do what I needed to do. Times when I didn't want to.

> I don't think I am up to this Lord.
> I don't have any energy left.
> *I will be your energy. Walk in my will.*
> My heart just isn't in this Father.
> I feel like I am faking it.

Walk in my will. I will change your heart.
It is so dark Jesus.

I can't see where to take the next step.
I will give you light for this step and
then I will give you light for the next one.
Walk in my will.
Father, why don't You make this stop?
Why have You let this happen?
Walk in my will. You will not be alone and
I promise, you will be blessed.

I have learned about God's faithfulness in the garden. He doesn't always remove the struggle, but He always carries me through. He is not a distant God who doesn't hear and doesn't care. He is "Abba." Do you know that this is the word for Daddy? When you find yourself in the garden again, hold onto Daddy's hand. He knows the way through.

Father, help me walk in Your will today.

What's In a Name?

You will also be a crown of beauty in the hand of the LORD,
And a royal diadem in the hand of your God.
It will no longer be said to you, "Forsaken,"
Nor to your land will it any longer be said, "Desolate";
But you will be called, "My delight is in her," . . .
For the LORD delights in you . . .
And as the bridegroom rejoices over the bride,
So your God will rejoice over you.

ISAIAH 62:3-5

I must confess that I experienced some serious resentment about having to carry my ex-husband's name after the divorce. At first I planned to take back my maiden name but my counselor advised me to reconsider. Because of the confusion it would cause my children, she encouraged me to try to find a way to live with it.

This wasn't always easy. It was particularly hard after my ex-husband remarried. Now there was a new Mrs. Hood and it wasn't me. So when one of my students called me "Mrs." instead of "Dr."

it drove me crazy! It wasn't because the "Dr." thing was a big deal to me. Many of my students call me by my first name. It was that each time I heard "Mrs. Hood," what I really heard was "forsaken, abandoned, and replaced."

Once again, the Lord had a message for me—a gift really. It was the night of my covenant group's annual Christmas party. We had started a new gift-giving tradition two or three years earlier. Instead of trading gifts we began trading scripture blessings. Each person comes to the party with a scripture blessing written on a piece of paper. We number them, put them in the center of the table, and randomly draw numbers just like we had with traditional presents. Then we read the scripture blessing aloud to the person who chooses our number.

It amazes us every year how God works in this simple tradition. Each person receives a word from the Lord that seems to have been chosen just for him or her. And on that year it was this scripture that the Lord, through my friend, gave me. He reminded me that my earthly name doesn't matter. My real name is "My delight is in her." And while my earthly bridegroom chose another bride, my eternal bridegroom rejoices over me. What a gift!

My dear Bridegroom,
remind me of my true name today.

DAY 22

Now I Get It!

My soul waits for the Lord more than the watchmen for the morning;
Indeed, more than the watchmen for the morning.

PSALM 130:6

When I was younger, I never got all those songs about heaven. You know, the songs that talked about how hard this life was and how much we looked forward to being at home with God. Songs about "farther along" and "flying away." I mean, heaven was going to be great and all, but things here aren't so bad. I sort of had the feeling that the people who wrote those songs needed to stop their bellyaching!

But now that I have lived a little more life, those songs make a lot more sense to me. I have watched friends watch their children die. Others have lost husbands to cancer. And I have walked through my own divorce and that of a dear friend. I gotta tell ya, now I get those old songs.

My soul does yearn now to be with God. I long to feel the comfort of His complete presence. Even though He does bless me in this life in more ways than I can count, I am now a lady in waiting. I wait and watch and hope—"more than watchmen for the morning."

Father, thank you for the blessings
of the here and now. But even more,
thank You for the promise of heaven.

Read the Instructions First

Thus says the LORD, your Redeemer, the Holy One of Israel,
I am the LORD your God, who teaches you to profit,
Who leads you in the way you should go.
If only you had paid attention to My commandments!
Then your well-being would have been like a river,
And your righteousness like the waves of the sea.

ISAIAH 48:17-18

A couple of months ago I spent about three hours trying to figure our how to program my CD player to play certain songs. I punched buttons and read the little numbers on the screen, but I just couldn't get it right. After a desperate search through the several places where I might have stored the manual, (Okay, paper work is not my best thing.) I remembered that my mom has a CD player just like mine. Knowing that she is a much better "filer" than I am, I called her up and asked her to find her instructions. In a matter of seconds, she had it. I quickly turned to the page marked

"Programming Instructions" and before you know it, I had done it. It is amazing what happens when you read the directions first.

Are you trying to live your life just figuring it out as you go? You don't have to. Our Manufacturer, our Maker, has given us the instructions. If we only take the time to seek His ways, He is faithful to guide us. Maybe you have lost contact with Him along the way. Find someone who can help you find your way back. He made you. He loves you. He wants what is best for you. He wants to make your well-being "like a river and your righteousness like the waves of the sea." Come on, pick up the manual. You will be amazed how much better life is when you read the instructions first.

Our Maker and Creator, thank You that You have not left us at the mercy of our own wisdom, but rather have given us Your word to light our paths.

DAY 24

I'll Change You

Create in me a clean heart, O God,
And renew a steadfast spirit within me.
Do not cast me away from Your presence
And do not take Your Holy Spirit from me.
Restore to me the joy of Your salvation
And sustain me with a willing spirit.

PSALM 51:10-11

It had been six months. Six months of waiting for my husband to decide whether he would stay or go. Living in the same house, but clearly not together. Six long months.

One night I was overcome with a sense of panic. "What if he decides to stay, but we live like this forever? What if he doesn't leave, but he doesn't change?"

Right then, I received a clear word from the Lord. "I'll change you," He said. An amazing peace came over me. I knew that no matter what happened, the Lord would "sustain me with a willing spirit."

He reminded me again that I cannot change anyone else. I cannot even change myself! That is His job. Philippians 2:13 reminds us that it is "God who is at work in you, both to will and to work for His good pleasure." Clean hearts are His business. Renewal is His department.

My husband did leave. But God has been faithful to His promise, changing me in many ways. He has taught me to trust Him, given me eyes to see the pain of others, and has restored my joy. And He will restore yours.

Father, here is my heart.
It could use a little clean-up.

DAY 25

By Name

LISTEN to Me, O islands, and pay attention,
you peoples from afar. The LORD called me from the womb;
from the body of my mother He named me.

ISAIAH 49:1

I am one of those impatient people who couldn't wait till my baby was born to find out if it was a boy or a girl. And as luck would have it, my son was in just the right position for us to be completely sure that he was a boy.

I loved knowing. I called him by his name. He was already a real person to me. When the nurses handed him to me in the delivery room, I took him in my arms and said, "Hello Wade," as if we had known each other forever.

We have a God who has known us forever. Long before the invention of sonograms, the Father has known His children before they were born. He calls them from their mothers' wombs. Rest in knowing that He called you. He is still calling. He knew you by name then and He knows you by name now. He has known you forever.

Precious Father, thank you for knowing me
and loving me anyway.

DAY 26

Stuck on the Mountain

I will lift up my eyes to the mountains;
From whence shall my help come?
My help comes from the LORD,
Who made heaven and earth.
He will not allow your foot to slip;
He who keeps you will not slumber.

PSALM 121:1-3

I have a tiny fear of heights. Well, maybe more than tiny. Okay, I am deathly afraid of heights. I love mountains—I just don't like standing too close to the edge.

It seems that every time I climb a steep hill or mountain I eventually find myself in a spot where I can't go any farther—not up or down, not left or right. Sure that I will slip right off the side of the mountain if I move, I am paralyzed. For a long time I crouch there in a panic wondering if I am going to be stuck there alone forever.

As I have walked through the death of my marriage there have been times when I have felt this same sense of panic. Not knowing which way to turn, uncertain about the future, feeling alone and abandoned like I am stuck on the side of a mountain, I have cried out to the source of my help.

I have learned that the Lord will always give me light for the next step. And when I trust Him with that tiny step, He gives me light for the next one. He will not let my foot slip.

Lord, help me trust you with each step I take today.

Engraved Forever

Can a woman forget her nursing child
And have no compassion on the son of her womb?
Even these may forget, but I will not forget you.
Behold, I have inscribed you on the palms of My hands;
Your walls are continually before Me.

ISAIAH 49:15-16

Even though I would never have the guts to get one, I must admit I kind of like some tattoos. I always wonder though, how that little rose is going to look on seventy-five-year-old skin. That thought and the fear of needles keep me far, far away from any tattoo parlor. I mean, it is so permanent. I love the little cartoon drawing of the man who keeps having old names scratched out and new names tattooed on until his arm is covered with one long list.

God has your name written on His hand. It is His forever tattoo. He will never mark through it. No matter who else scratches you off their list to make room for another name, your name will forever be inscribed in the hand of the Father. That is His promise and His promises are true.

Next time you feel alone and abandoned by God, look down at the palm of your hand. Imagine that you are looking at the hand of God with your name written there on His palm. You are not forgotten. You are continually before Him.

Faithful Father, thank you that
you will never forget me.

DAY 28

Is That Your Final Answer?

One of the scribes came and heard them arguing,
and recognizing that He had answered them well, asked Him,
"What commandment is the foremost of all?"

MARK 12:28

Throughout Jesus' ministry, people asked him questions. Some wanted something from Him. Others wanted Him to explain something He had said. Some questions were meant to trap Him and some even to rebuke Him. But again and again people were amazed at His answers. From the time He was twelve-years-old in the temple, He awed people with His insight and authority.

And so it was with this man. He saw that Jesus had answered well and so he came with his own question—a central question about central truth. As we read on we find that this man had great understanding of the heart of God. What he didn't understand is that, not only did Jesus know the answers, Jesus was the answer.

What are the questions of your heart? Do you wonder if your life will have meaning? Jesus is the answer. Perhaps you are confused about suffering and pain. Jesus is the answer. Are you searching for the place where you will finally find "true love?" Jesus is the answer.

We live in a world that is uncertain and always changing and so many people have decided that there are no answers. There is no truth. But the truth is that for all the questions in this world that really matter, the answer is not a concept, a theory or an idea. The answer is a person. The final answer is Jesus.

Jesus, thank you for accepting me in my
confusion and with all my questions. Help me rest
in knowing that You are my answer.

DAY 29

Looking Back

And there arose a fierce gale of wind, and the waves were breaking over the boat so much that the boat was already filling up. Jesus Himself was in the stern, asleep on the cushion; and they woke Him and said to Him, "Teacher, do You not care that we are perishing?"

MARK 4:37-38

Have you ever wondered if Jesus had forgotten you? You are in the middle of a storm—a divorce, a lost job, the grief of death, an illness—and you wonder where Jesus is. And like these men you cry out, "Don't you even care?"

I have been there. Like these men I had seen Jesus work powerfully in my life, but when the waves got too big I felt abandoned. But the story doesn't end there. With a quiet, gentle command Jesus stilled the storm. Perhaps the apostles had to live through the storm to understand more deeply this man they had already left everything to follow.

My divorce is the biggest storm I have ever faced. I have been shaken and afraid. There are times when I have felt that Jesus was far away. But looking back I can see the powerful and gentle ways that He carried me through. I have come to know Him better during these 2 1/2 years than in all the other years of my life combined.

Next time you find yourself in a storm, hold onto Jesus. Cry out when you feel lost and alone. And when the storm passes, don't forget to look back. You will discover that He was there all the time.

Precious Jesus, speak your peace into my heart.

DAY 30

Unspeakable Words

Why do You stand afar off, O LORD?
Why do You hide Yourself in times of trouble?

PSALM 10:1

I saw a friend the other day whose marriage is in desperate trouble. "I've prayed and prayed," she said. "Does God not care about life here? Does He only care about the life after this?" I held her hand and asked, "Have you read the Psalms lately?"

About a week later we ran into each other again. She told me that she had opened her Bible to the Psalms that very night after we talked and she was amazed. All the things she felt were written right there.

In the Psalms the Father gives us the words to speak the unspeakable. The Psalms call us to be honest with God and with each other. There is no sugar-coating there. Struggles are real and questions are hard.

Our God is big enough for whatever we bring Him. Run to Him with your anger, your confusion, and your questions. The struggles do not mean you don't have faith. The struggle is part of the faith. And guess what? The feelings, the fears that you have—He's heard it before. He understands. He knows. You can tell Him anything.

Father, here I am with all my anger, confusion, and fear. Help me to trust you with all my feelings.

DAY 31

Forgetful Father

As far as the east is from the west,
So far has He removed our transgressions from us.

PSALM 103:12

I didn't want a divorce. That was my ex-husband's choice. He didn't want counseling. He didn't want to talk. He didn't want me. He just wanted out. So he left.

It would be easy for me to be self-righteous. After all, I tried. I went to counseling. I wanted to save our marriage. So it would be easy for me to see myself as the innocent victim. That is, if I didn't remember. Remember the times I was impatient or selfish. The times I failed to love unconditionally.

The enemy would love to see the guilt of past mistakes swallow me up. He whispers in my ear to remind me of all the times I messed up. He loves that I remember. But what Satan hates is that God does not remember. "As far as the east is from the west." That is how far those memories are from our forgetful Father.

Yes, confess your mistakes. Seek God's power to change. But don't hold on to those memories. Lay them down at the foot of the cross. Walk away into a new life. He has removed your transgressions from you.

Father, help me give you my past so that
I can walk into Your future.

DAY 32

Trust Me

For My thoughts are not your thoughts,
Nor are your ways My ways, declares the LORD.
For as the heavens are higher than the earth,
So are My ways higher than your ways
And My thoughts than your thoughts.

ISAIAH 55:8-9

I had a wonderful childhood. I even look back on adolescence fondly. It may sound strange, but I was never embarrassed by my parents. They always seemed pretty cool to me. Perhaps this was because they always respected my point of view. My sisters and I knew that any topic was open for discussion. I could ask any question and know that my parents would answer if they could.

This doesn't mean that they let us do whatever we wanted. Absolutely not! But they usually gave us reasons for the decisions they made. Every once in a while though, my dad would say, "I don't think I can explain this to you. I just don't feel good about it. So you are just going to have to trust me on this one when I say no." When Daddy said this, I never argued. He had shown himself again and again to be trustworthy. I had no doubt that he wanted what was best for me. So when he asked me to trust him without explanation, I did.

Perhaps this is why I love the mystery of God. Some people are bothered by it. They are troubled by some of the things God does and some of the things He chooses not to do. When I am confronted by a situation like this, I remember what my earthly father used to say and I can imagine the same words coming from my Heavenly Father. "I don't think I can explain this to you. You are just going to have to trust me." See, He has shown Himself to be trustworthy again and again. And I have no doubt that He wants what is best for me. He wants what is best for you too. You are just going to have to trust Him on that.

Father of mystery, help me to trust you
when things don't make sense.

DAY 33

Shattered Plates

Cast your burden upon the LORD and He will sustain you;
He will never allow the righteous to be shaken.

PSALM 55:22

I awoke that morning with a terrible ache in my right arm. Did I just sleep on it wrong? Did I pull something? Then I remembered, "Oh, yeah! I threw about 100 plates into that ravine yesterday."

It was my anniversary and my husband had just moved out. A friend of mine has a special place on her ranch called the "wailing wall"—a tall solid rock wall in a secluded ravine. My friends took me there with stacks of plates from garage sales, junk stores, and a few from my wedding china. They prayed over me and left me there alone with the Lord. I shattered plate after plate against the ravine wall. I cried out to God, screamed at Satan, and shouted at my husband. I . . . well, I wailed.

Later that day I opened my prayer journal to write about this horrible, holy, healing experience. There at the bottom of the page was this scripture, "Cast your burden upon the LORD . . ."

Do you have a few burdens you need to cast the Father's way? Whether you need to scream, cry, or throw a plate or two, He is waiting for you. Waiting to sustain you. He will not let you be shaken.

Father, help me to depend on you
to carry my burdens today.

DAY 34

Faithful Friends

Being unable to get to Him because of the crowd,
they removed the roof above Him;
and when they had dug an opening,
they let down the pallet on which the paralytic was
lying. And Jesus seeing their faith said to the paralytic,
"Son, your sins are forgiven."

MARK 2:4-5

As a little girl, I always heard this story told in a very matter of fact way. But I couldn't help wondering about the people who owned the house. How did they feel about this new skylight in their ceiling? Were the roofs in Bible times built with easily removable holes? The little cardboard model in my second grade Bible class had a special section in the roof that just came right off. But I seriously doubt that real houses were made this way.

These men were obviously determined to get their friend to Jesus. They wouldn't be stopped by crowds or by brick and mortar.

Why were they so tenacious? It's because they knew Jesus had the power to heal. Their friend would be fine if they could just get him to this man. They believed this completely, and so they did not give up.

The people there that day only understood part of Jesus' healing power. They had seen Him heal the blind and make all kinds of sick people well. But they didn't understand his power to heal spiritually. Jesus tried on that day to help them see that His greatest power was that over sin.

I, on the other hand, know the rest of the story. Jesus conquered death and so He conquered sin. I know that only through Him can we experience the ultimate healing. Thinking about these faithful friends makes me ask myself, "How desperate am I to help the people I know find true healing?" I'm not sure I like the answer.

Jesus, help me have a sense of urgency about
bringing people to you.

DAY 35

A New Normal

I would have despaired unless I had believed that I would see the
goodness of the LORD in the land of the living. Wait for the LORD;
Be strong and let your heart take courage; yes, wait for the LORD.

PSALM 27:13-14

She looked at me with tears streaming down her face.
"Mommy, things will never be normal again." Her father had just
moved out and her eight-year-old heart was breaking. Mine broke
right along with her.

"Sweetie, God will give us a new normal," I said. "You will
always, always be sad about this, but God will give us joy too." I
opened my Bible and read this scripture for her. We wrote it on a
big piece of paper, hung it over her bed, and prayed these words
every night for several months

That was almost nine years ago and, yes, the sadness is still
there. But God has been faithful to His promise. Our new home has
become home. We have made some wonderful new family

memories. The Lord has taught us so much about trusting Him. We have seen His goodness, even through these tough times.

You can trust this promise too. Cling to it when things look hopeless. Pray these words to remind your broken heart to take courage. And then watch. He is faithful. Things will never be the same, but there are blessings waiting for you. You can count on it.

Father, help me to trust, to wait, and to watch.

Day 36

Come Away

And He said to them, "Come away by yourselves to a secluded place
and rest a while." (For there were many people coming and
going, and they did not even have time to eat.)

MARK 6:31

I remember a trip to Disney World when I was a little girl.
Along with the magical wonders of "It's a Small World" and "20,000
Leagues Under the Sea" was an exhibit on the future of technology.
A mysterious, all-knowing expert voice guided us through the mind-
boggling display. This voice declared that when these futuristic
gadgets become reality, they will make work more fast and efficient
and we will have more time for leisure.

Well, here we are, more years than I care to mention later, and
many of these "gadgets" are now a reality. Most of us have cell
phones, e-mail, and of course, the internet. I don't know about you,
but my life doesn't seem to be slowing down. It seems to be
speeding up.

Be honest. Have you had a day lately when you "did not even have time to eat?" Jesus is calling you to come away. Be quiet. Rest. Listen. Relax. No need to feel guilty. It is an invitation from the Master.

Father of peace, help me learn to be still
and know that You are God.

DAY 37

Looking Ahead

Brethren, I do not regard myself as having laid hold of it yet;
but one thing I do: forgetting what lies behind and reaching forward to
what lies ahead, press on toward the goal for the prize
of the upward call of God in Christ Jesus.

PHILIPPIANS 3:13-14

The frustrating thing about divorce is that it has a way of stealing your past as well as changing your future. After my divorce I couldn't seem to look back on even the happy times in my marriage with sentimental nostalgia. Those happier days seemed to take on the grief of brokenness and the memories brought confusion. "What was that? Was it real? Did he still love me then? Did he ever love me?" So the past was gone and the future was . . . well, uncertain.

I found myself having to reframe everything—every holiday, every birthday, every family trip, everything! One time in particular stands out in my mind. It was time for our church family retreat. My children wanted to go. The only problem was that my husband

and I had at one time been in charge of this annual retreat. It was one of the rare places where we served in ministry together. The thought of going as a single-again struck a fear in me that I cannot describe, but my children wanted to go.

So, we packed the van, invited some friends, and struck out toward the Texas Hill Country. I prayed the entire four-hour trip down and when we drove into the campsite I thought I was going to unravel. Thankfully, my children ran off with friends to claim their bunks in the cabins and I had some time alone. I ran off too, quite literally. I ran until I found a place far away from anyone, crumpled to the ground and cried out. "Lord, it was wrong to come! I can't spend three days here! I can't! Everywhere I look is a memory and you know how I feel about memories!"

I felt his gentle hand as he said, "Leave what is behind, Dana. Press on!" So with a deep breath and the strength of the Father I did press on. I unpacked. I hiked. I played dominoes. I sang. I visited. I even laughed. By the end of the retreat I realized that God had redeemed this special event. I experienced that weekend the God who truly makes all things new! He will do this for you too.

Lord, remove from me whatever is keeping me in
the past and help me press on!

DAY 38

Enough is Enough

*And His disciples answered Him, "Where will anyone be able to find
enough bread here in this desolate place to satisfy these people?"*

MARK 8:4

This is one of those stories that make me look at Bible charac-
ters and ask, "How stupid are they?" Weren't these the same guys
who were with Jesus when He fed the 5000 with 5 loaves and two
fish? Here they are in almost the exact same situation and they still
don't get it. Thinking it is up to them, they still worry that they do
not have enough.

But when I step back a little, I realize that I am no different. I
look at what I bring Jesus and think it isn't enough. What, me, teach
that class? I don't know enough and besides, my life is not together
enough. An hour a week is not enough time to make a difference in
the lives of children. I really don't have enough experience with
that. I don't think I could say anything that would help.

Then I think about stories like this one and I ask myself, "How stupid am I?" God never did need enough. He didn't need a tall, strong soldier to defeat Goliath. He needed a shepherd boy. He made a serious point of not needing enough with Gideon. All he wanted was a few men with torches and pots. And he didn't need enough to feed these people in the wilderness. It is not about me having enough. The point is that I know the One who is enough.

So the next time you are tempted to say that you don't have enough, stop! Give what little you do have to Jesus and watch what He will do. I think you will be amazed.

Father, remind me that You are sufficient
for me. And by the way, here are a few loaves and
fish that You can use if you like.

DAY 39

The God of the Sea

For I am the LORD your God, who stirs up the sea and
its waves roar (the LORD of hosts is His name).

ISAIAH 51:15

Where do you like to go to feel really close to God? Some people I know are mountain people. They love to look out from the heights and see God's world stretch out before them. The majesty of the mountains makes them feel the presence of God.

I too love the mountains. But the real place for me is the ocean. It is powerful and yet peaceful. The waves are constant and sure. Within its depths are mysteries beyond our reach. The ocean is for me an awesome testimony to God's presence and power.

So what am I doing living in West Texas? The closest thing we have to an ocean is a big red lake that is almost dry now. But even so, I remember. I can close my eyes and see its crashing waves. I can hear it and smell it. Even when I can't see the ocean, I know it is there.

And so it is with God. He is constant and sure—powerful and yet peaceful. His mysteries are beyond our imagination. And even when your life looks more like West Texas, you can place your trust in the one "who stirs up the sea . . . the LORD of hosts is His name."

Sovereign Lord, I place my trust in You.

DAY 40

True Holy Moments

And He took them in His arms and
began blessing them, laying His hands on them.

MARK 10: 16

When you picture this scene, do you imagine a serene moment—angelic children gazing with awe into Jesus' eyes? Is there a soft glow surrounding them reminiscent of the soft-lens filming of beautiful women in old movies? All the children are perfectly behaved and reverent—a holy moment.

If this is how you imagine it, perhaps you need to visit a three-year-old Bible class. Go to a playground. Hang out in an elementary school lunchroom. And as you watch, imagine the children right in front of you climbing into Jesus' lap. Does it change your picture a little?

My guess is that if it were a scene like we often see in paintings, the apostles might not have been so upset. After all, this was Jesus and Jesus is serious business. Surely He didn't have time for wiggly bodies, runny noses, silly jokes, and childish questions. But the apostles didn't get it. Jesus understood that giggles and hugs from children are serious business. Sloppy kisses may not make for a real serene picture, but they are true holy moments.

Father, thank you for a Savior who saw the holiness in the simple and ordinary things in life— a Savior who even had time for children.

DAY 41

Fearfully and Wonderfully Made

For You formed my inward parts;
You wove me in my mother's womb.
I will give thanks to You, for I am fearfully and wonderfully made;
Wonderful are Your works,
And my soul knows it very well.

PSALM 139:13-14

A dear friend of mine recently had a big surprise. At almost 40, with a sixteen-year-old daughter, she was going to be a mother again. Oops!

It was a difficult pregnancy with about three months in bed. But finally he arrived. You have never seen such silliness as all my forty something friends oohed and aahed at this little wonder. I held him in my arms and could not stop the tears. He was "fearfully and wonderfully made!"

It is easy for us to see the wonder in a little baby, but somehow as we grow older we forget. We become dissatisfied with who and what we are. We don't measure up to the world's standards. And for those of us who have suffered the pain of divorce, it is easy to feel quite a bit less than wonderful.

But we all began as that little baby. We were all formed by the Father and we are His masterpiece. The wonder of who we are, as people made in the very image of God, has not faded because we have gotten older. You are fearfully and wonderfully made—one of the Father's greatest treasures. Believe it!

Father, help me look to You today
to determine my value.

DAY 42

Gift of Love

"She has done what she could; she has anointed My body beforehand for the burial. Truly I say to you, wherever the gospel is preached in the whole world, what this woman has done will also be spoken of in memory of her."

MARK 14:8-9

Wow! To have Jesus say words like this about me, I can't imagine it. I'm pretty sure that the men there on that day were pretty amazed too—and not necessarily in a good way. This was a waste of money. And besides, who was she anyway. She was just some woman. But Jesus accepted this woman's "silly" gift. And He didn't just accept it, He honored her.

I love this story; not just because I am a woman myself, although that is part of it. I love it because it gives us a window into the heart of Jesus. You see, women at this time were second class citizens. They were often dismissed, at the mercy of men. But Jesus treated them with honor and respect. He didn't let the culture of

His day dictate how He would treat people. He saw the value in people whom the world at that time dismissed and rejected.

It gives me hope. I don't have to be important or smart to come to Jesus. I just have to come, give Him what I have, and do what I can. He takes care of the rest. I know that some day I will look into the eyes of my sweet Savior and He will smile at me lovingly as I imagine He did at her. What gift could I possibly give Him to deserve that? You're right. Nothing.

Sweet Jesus, thank you that your love is not reserved for the important of this world. Thank you for loving the unimportant ones like me.

DAY 43

God's Sea Showcase

O LORD, how many are Your works! In wisdom You have made them all;
The earth is full of Your possessions. There is the sea, great and broad, in
which are swarms without number, animals both small and great.

PSALM 104:24-25

I have a thing for aquariums. Not those little ones that fit in your living room. Those are cool, but what I am talking about is those really big ones that you have to pay money to see. Whenever I am in a city with an aquarium, I do everything I can to go.

There is nothing like it to remind me of the awesome wonder of my God. I revel in His power and His sometimes, playful creativity as I wander through each exhibit. There are fish that can change gender depending on the needs of the population, animals that remind me of funny little pink plants you might find in a Dr. Seuss book, seahorses that look just like floating leaves, and tiny translucent jellyfish dancing around like bits of lace. At the aquarium you discover that florescent colors were God's idea.

But you don't really have to go to a fancy aquarium to see the works of our Father. They are all around you. Spend some time today basking in the glory of God's creation. You might be surprised at how it will renew your spirit.

Oh Lord, how many are Your works!
Help me not to miss a single one today.

DAY 44

Just as He Told You

"But go, tell His disciples and Peter, He is going ahead of you to Galilee; there you will see Him, just as He told you."

MARK 16:7

Don't you love this gentle reminder from the angel? "Remember, He told you this was going to happen." This wasn't, as I see it, one of those "I told you so's" that we all hate to get. I believe it was the Lord's way to say to the disciples, "Jesus told you He would die and then rise in three days. I know you thought this was crazy at the time. You didn't understand. It didn't make sense. But now you see. If Jesus says something, it is so. You can count on that." And so they learned that if they could trust Jesus with this amazing, unbelievable thing, they could trust Him with anything.

Jesus said He would never leave them, that He would always love them and that He was going to prepare a place for them. No matter what they had done in the past, He promised to forgive. He would be their strength. They would be His brothers and sisters. These things would happen, just as He told them.

We can trust these words too. Sometimes life doesn't make sense. At times it may seem crazy to follow Jesus. There is so much we don't understand. But this we know. We have a Savior who has conquered death, just as He said He would. And if He can come through on that promise, we can take Him at His word. When Jesus says something, it is so. You can count on that!

Faithful Father, help me rest in knowing that
You always keep your promises.

DAY 45

Real Beauty

For the LORD takes pleasure in His people;
He will beautify the afflicted ones with salvation.

PSALM 149:4

I finally did it. After having my gray pointed out to me one too many times, I colored my hair. My nineteen-year-old niece told me it would change my life. So far the biggest change I can see is that every five weeks I have to go back and do it again! My new life as a blond has simply been more expensive.

Don't get me wrong. I do like the way my hair looks and I enjoy the compliments I have received. It has given me a nice little boost. But it has not changed my life—at least not in ways that really matter.

After years of trying to please my husband, wanting him to find me beautiful, he left. That rejection made me feel unworthy, unwanted, and unloved. I was definitely what you would call an "afflicted one."

Then, I read words like these and my broken heart was touched in ways I cannot describe. The God of the universe takes pleasure in me. Can that be true? He rejoices over me. He "beautifies me with salvation." Try buying that at your local hair salon.

Father, help me rest in knowing that
true beauty comes from you.
Give me eyes to see that beauty in others.

DAY 46

Where is Your Egypt?

WOE to those who go down to Egypt for help and rely on horses,
and trust in chariots because they are many and in horsemen
because they are very strong, but they do not look to
the Holy One of Israel, nor seek the LORD!

ISAIAH 31:1

Recently our church finished a study of the book of Genesis. It was amazing to see how often God's people seemed to go to Egypt. Even after the Hebrew slaves were rescued from slavery, they wanted to go back. Egypt had a strength they could see and touch. If they weren't happy, at least they were secure.

We have our "Egypts" too—places, people and things that make us feel safe and secure. Things that help us escape from our troubles. Things like food, television, work, and even friends. Oddly enough, these things aren't bad in themselves. It is how we use them that matters.

There were even times when God sent people to Egypt. Joseph was told to take Mary and the baby Jesus to Egypt to escape the wrath of an evil king. So there are times to run to friends when we are in trouble and even times to escape into a good book. But eventually we learn that God is the only One we can truly rely on. He may use things we can touch and see to make His presence known, but in the end our trust must be in Him—the Holy One of Israel.

Father, take me out of Egypt.
I place my trust in You.

DAY 47

Searching For One

And He looked around to see the woman who had done this.
But the woman fearing and trembling, aware of what had happened to
her, came and fell down before Him and told Him the whole truth.
And He said to her, "Daughter, your faith has made you well;
go in peace and be healed of your affliction."

MARK 5:32-34

I love stories that give me a picture of the heart of Jesus. This is one of those stories. Jesus stopped to find this one woman who had touched Him. His followers thought it was outrageous. How could he possibly know if He had been touched? Everyone was touching Him. Among this pressing crowd, how could He expect to find one person?

But He did find her. He looked in her eyes and calmed her fear. Her body had already been healed. Jesus knew she needed more. She needed comfort. She needed hope. She needed Him.

We don't have a Savior who dispenses healing from a distance. He wants us to understand that He knows us—that He wants us to know Him. He wants to affirm our faith, heal our pain, and give us hope. He wants us to look into His eyes and know that we are truly loved—not as a thronging crowd, but as one unique person.

Jesus, thank you for looking
through the crowds to find me.

DAY 48

Different People–Same God!

Behold, how good and how pleasant it is for brothers to
dwell together in unity! It is like the precious oil upon the head.

PSALM 133:1-2

I looked around the room at the women gathered there and thought, "This really shouldn't work." Here we were—widows and wives; singles and singles again; millionaires and school teachers; army captains and homemakers. What could possibly bring this odd assortment of women together?

The answer—prayer. This group of women with different lifestyles, different childhoods and from different religious denominations comes together once a week to pray. There as we kneel in my friend's living room, our differences matter very little. We are all one at the foot of the cross.

There is something unifying about praying honestly with someone. We find that for all our differences, we are really very much the same. We learn that grief is grief. Whether it is the grief of divorce, death of a loved one, or the pain of caring for aging parents, we all need the strength of the Father and the arms of a friend to face each day.

Do you have a place where you can share and pray honestly with someone? If not, perhaps you need to be that place for someone else. Then, guess what? You will have a place too.

Father, thank you for the gift of community.
Help me be a safe place for someone today.

DAY 49

Victory from Failure

May those who wait for You not be ashamed through me,
O Lord GOD of hosts; may those who seek You
not be dishonored through me, O God of Israel.

PSALM 69:6

I teach in a Christian university. I take very seriously my responsibility to nurture young men and women in faith. My prayer is that my students will see in my life the faith I profess.

After my divorce, I was afraid to let my students know. Will this destroy my witness? Will it confuse their faith? Will I bring dishonor to God because my marriage has failed? At that time I prayed this Psalm over and over.

What a surprise God had in store for me! Once again I learned that my circumstances do not limit what He can do through me. My patient Father taught me again (I am a slow learner.) that His strength is made perfect through weakness. The Lord has used me in the lives of my students in ways I could have never imagined.

Have you let the deceiver convince you that the Father no longer has any use for you? Don't believe it! We serve a God who can turn mourning into dancing. He can bring victory from failure. And he can use broken people to bring his healing power to the world.

Father, thank you for removing my shame.
Here is my imperfect life.
Use it for your glory today.

DAY 50

"I Am Here!"

When I consider Your heavens, the work of Your fingers,
The moon and the stars, which You have ordained;
What is man that You take thought of him,
And the son of man that You care for him?

PSALM 8:3-4

I got out of bed very early that morning before the sun rose. I can't really tell you why. Well, now I know why. The Lord had some serious teaching to do. I had been wrapped up in my frustrations and struggles. Holding on to the things this world has to offer to "make it through." I didn't have time for Bible study. I was too tired to pray. And I wondered why things were so hard. And so God nudged, okay he pushed me out of bed that morning to teach me a little lesson.

I figured that I was awake already, so I might at least use the time in some productive way. I put on my walking shoes and headed out the door for some exercise. When I opened the door I heard myself gasp. There it was right in front of me—the biggest, blue-black velvet sky full of stars. And I knew.

While I was trying to take care of the things in my life on my own, He was there. The God of the universe was mindful of me and I had been ignoring him. The Creator of the heavens was waiting to take my frustrations and my struggles and I was trying to work things out on my own. God shouted at me through that beautiful starry sky. "I am here! Let it go!"

I did go for a long walk that morning. But I understood in a new way that I didn't walk alone. The one who placed the stars in the sky walked with me. He walks with me still. And like the Psalmist, I am amazed!

King of the heavens, I place my trust in you.
I am letting go!

DAY 51

Such is the Kingdom Moments

A joyful heart is good medicine, but a broken spirit dries up the bones.

PROVERBS 17:22

For more than twenty years I have been teaching kindergarten Bible class on Sunday mornings. After all this time I don't know if I would know how to act in a grown-up Bible class. I mean adult Bible classes have no crayons or markers. They don't jump up and down when they sing songs. There are no storybooks or crafts. And I think I would really miss those things.

But this isn't why I stay with the children. I stay because they teach me great truths about God. I call these lessons "such as the kingdom" moments—moments when the kingdom breaks in through the words of a child.

When he came to the front of the class for sharing time on that Sunday morning, I had no idea that this would be one of those kingdom moments. All I saw was the cast on his arm. Immediately I began asking about the cast. I assumed that this was what he wanted to share.

He patiently answered all my questions. His arm was broken during his first ever soccer practice. Yes, it had hurt a lot. They did go to the emergency room. He would be in a cast for a while. Sleeping was a little difficult. He was so patient with my endless curiosity.

Finally I asked him, "Did you want to share today about your broken arm?" His eyes got big and he broke out in a big smile. "No, I have really good news to share! I am on a soccer team!"

I had to laugh. Here he was with a broken arm from his very first soccer practice and rather than complaining he wanted to celebrate being part of a team. Now this is a "glass half full" kind of kid. I saw in him the gift of a joyful heart. It was indeed good medicine—for him and for me.

Father, help me to choose a joyful heart today.

DAY 52

Unexpected Fulfillment

I will cry to God Most High, to God who accomplishes all things for me.

PSALM 57:2

I looked forward to our lunches together. She encouraged and challenged my faith like no one else. She had a way of asking probing questions that I felt compelled to answer. On that day it wasn't a question that she had for me. She had prayed that God would give her some words for me. She said, "All your dreams for what you will do in the kingdom will be fulfilled."

I felt affirmed by God and I trusted that promise. Then eighteen months later, when my marriage fell apart, I thought it was all over.

The deceiver wanted me to believe that because I was broken, God could no longer use me. How wrong I was! It was because I was broken that He was able to fulfill that promise. This devotional that you are reading—well, it is part of that fulfillment.

This isn't because I am special. It is the Father who "accomplishes all things for me." And He can accomplish in your life what He has planned for you—perhaps not what you expected. (I didn't expect to write about divorce.) But it will be His perfect plan. Trust that.

Father, help me to walk according to your plans
today and not my own.

DAY 53

I Am Still Here!

And lo, I am with you always, even to the end of the age."
MATTHEW 28:20 (NASB)

Forty families from our church had spent a week in ministry in Itu, Brazil. My little family of three was part of the team. It was the second time we had traveled to Brazil on a mission trip and it was the second time that I was the only single parent on the mission trip.

It was an amazing week! God worked in ways we could never have planned ourselves. Each person's gifts were used through Bible studies, Vacation Bible School, special seminars, counseling, construction projects, a youth camp, and a concert. It was a busy week.

As is often the tradition on mission trips like this, we ended the week with a day of recreation. We spent an entire day shopping, driving, hiking, driving, dining, driving and exploring. Did I mention driving? It was a busy day. That evening when we all climbed back on the buses to head back to the hotel we were all exhausted. The kids gathered in the back and talked and laughed quietly. The adults took the opportunity for a much needed nap.

Couples sat together. Husbands and wives. Heads on shoulders. Arms around each other. And I was alone. No shoulder to lean on. No arms to hold me. No husband. Alone in my seat, turned my face to the cold window and wept silently.

I wondered if God had forgotten me. I had come on this trip as the only single parent. Did anyone understand how hard this was for me? Did they even care? Did God? I guess you can see that I was having a serious "pitty party."

When we got up the next morning I was still feeling quite sorry for myself. As we were gathering to get back on the bus my friend Susan pulled me aside and said, "Dana, I have been wanting to tell you that I really respect you for coming on this trip as a single parent. I can imagine that it would be a very hard thing to do."

These simple words blessed me more than I can say. They were a reminder. He will never leave me. I was not alone on that bus. My Savior was there—a shoulder to lean on and arms to hold me. As the tears rolled down my cheeks that night, He saw me. My sweet friend was His voice saying, "No matter where you are, Dana, I am there."

Those words are for you too. He sees you in those dark and lonely times. He knows your heartache. You are not alone. Take the simple words I have written in this book as your reminder. You are cherished. He is there. "Even to the end of the age."

As you close this book, choose to be His voice for someone else. Remind them and you will remind yourself. The Savior is not far off. He is here. A shoulder to lean on and arms to hold you. His is with you always!

God's Blessings,
Dana

Divorce Recovery Resources

"Radical Recovery is a resource guide to help you survive those first awful days, weeks, months, and, of course, all the nights of a mid-life divorce. But the goal is not just survival, it's life-transformation. In spite of your divorce, there is a destiny for you beyond your wildest dreams. Believe that truth and get your new life started today."

THE AUTHOR

"Radical Recovery will shake you out of your lethargy, knock you out of your bitterness, and bounce you out of your self-pity parties. If you want something that is pie-in-the-sky and full of pleasant theories, skip this book. If you want to get better, you have come to the right text."

DAN KNIGHT, OVERLAND PARK CHURCH OF CHRIST, OVERLAND PARK, KANSAS

Radical Recovery
Transforming the Despair of Your Divorce into an Unexpected Good
224 pages $15.99
ISBN 978-0-89112-518-1

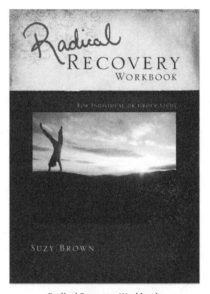

Radical Recovery Workbook
64 pages $9.99
ISBN 978-0-89112-508-2

LEAFWOOD
P U B L I S H E R S
www.leafwoodpublishers.com

1·877·816·4455

SUZY BROWN conducts divorce recovery workshops and hosts a website: www.midlifedivorcerecovery.com.

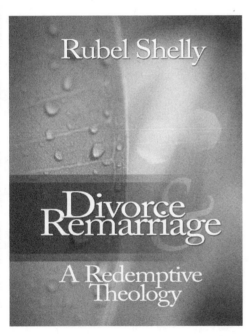